RESISTANCE

RESISTANCE

A Memoir of Civil Disobedience in Maricopa County

Annette S. Marquis

Skinner House Books
Boston

www.skinnerhouse.org

Printed in the United States

print ISBN: 978-1-55896-713-7
eBook ISBN: 978-1-55896-697-0

6 5 4 3 2 1
15 14 13

To the women and men
of the civil rights movement,
who taught us so much about
the power of non-violent resistance.

CONTENTS

ACKNOWLEDGMENTS

———◆———

The act of civil disobedience can be terrifying for the lone activist who chooses to put their body on the line against injustice. My experience of civil disobedience in Phoenix on July 29, 2010, differed in an important way. Immigrant justice partner groups, Unitarian Universalist Association staff and volunteer leaders, civil disobedience trainers, volunteers and staff from local UU congregations, attorneys, and others I don't even know wrapped me in a blanket of support and carried me on their shoulders through the fear.

I extend my deepest appreciation to each person who participated in planning the actions that took place that day. I cannot name everyone so I will name those I can and ask them to extend my thanks to those I fail to mention.

Thank you, first of all, to Rev. Susan Frederick-Gray. You called for us to come and because of your leadership and your courage, many of us chose to follow. Your congregation, the Unitarian Universalist Congregation of Phoenix, as well as Valley Unitarian Universalist

Congregation and individual UUs in the Phoenix area welcomed us and cared for us while we were there. And thank you, Rev. Peter Morales, president of the Unitarian Universalist Association, who answered the call and encouraged others to come with you.

The people of Puente Arizona, our partners in this work, were there since before the beginning. They might have been surprised by how many "yellow-shirts" turned out, but made sure we were well taken care of in many ways, especially with legal support through the incredible pro-bono work of Navidad, Leal, and Silva. Thank you all.

Rev. Ken Brown, district executive of the Pacific Southwest District, played a critical role in planning and supporting our actions and managing the aftermath. Thank you, Ken. You are no stranger to civil disobedience and your experience and insight helped those of us who never had the courage before.

Thank you, Susan Leslie, Audra Friend, and Dan Furmansky, who mobilized UUs across the country, connected the national staff to the district and local organizers, and handled countless behind-the-scenes details to make everything run smoothly. And thank you, Emrys Stanton and Sandy Weir, who offered local on-the-ground support.

Thank you, Gini Courter, moderator of the Unitarian Universalist Association. The vigil you organized outside the jail reverberated inside and gave us courage over the long night, and you made sure a crowd was there to cheer us on our release. That and the many other things you did made a huge difference.

Chris Crass and others from the Catalyst Project, including my old friend Betty Jeanne Reuters-Ward and people from the Ruckus Society, trained and prepared us for what it means to engage in civil disobedience, helped with planning the actions, and showed us how to work with local police. They were all invaluable.

For every one of us who spent time in Sheriff Joe's jail, countless others fretted by the phone. They not only supported our decisions, but loved us in spite of, and in some cases, because of them. For me that starts with my wife, Wendy DeGroat, who never asked why, only how she could help.

I extend my thanks to Rev. Jeanne Pupke, who lit the fire in me to go to Arizona and backed me every step of the way. To Rev. Elaine Peresluha, who said yes when I asked her to be my official support person—seeing you on the phone with Wendy when I stepped into the police van allowed me to breathe again. To Julian Sharpe, who snapped my arrest photos and took some of my stuff back to the church for me. Especially to the women who shared the experience with me—your songs, jokes, prayers, and love made it possible to endure even the hardest moments, when violence brushed us much too closely. And to the men who donned pink but didn't let Sheriff Joe's humiliation tactics break your resolve.

You are all my heroes.

ARREST

---✦---

July 29, 2010, 10:22 a.m. Even in the early morning hours, the Arizona sun had scorched us as we marched from Trinity Episcopal Cathedral to Cesar Chavez Plaza in Phoenix. I now stand with hundreds of other protestors, baking in that sun, at the intersection of Washington Street and First Avenue in downtown Phoenix. I'm sure it has to be at least 120 degrees out here. Sweat trickles down my chest and back and pools at the waistband of my pants. Fortunately, I had stopped at a sporting goods store last night and bought a lightweight white golf cap. ClimaCool, it is called. I can't say it is keeping me cool, but at least sweat isn't dripping down my face as well. In addition to my protective hat, I am a wearing a bright, goldenrod-colored T-shirt with the logo and motto of the Standing on the Side of Love (SSL) campaign, a public witness program of my faith community, the Unitarian Universalist Association. My arms are linked firmly at the elbow with two other protestors, so if the hat doesn't do its job, there is no way I can wipe the sweat from my face.

Today is the day Arizona enacts its latest anti-immigration legislation, SB 1070, commonly referred to as the "Papers, Please" law. This law requires everyone, American citizen or not, to carry identification papers or risk being arrested as an illegal alien. As a middle-class, white woman of Irish, French, and German descent, I know police will never stop me and ask me for my papers. They target only people of darker skin, people who do not speak English as a primary language, people who, according to the police, "look" illegal. Systematically targeting and arresting people because they fit a profile of an illegal immigrant violates the first of the seven Principles of Unitarian Universalism, which affirms "the inherent worthy and dignity of every person." This egregious violation of human rights prompted me to decide, along with scores of other Unitarian Universalists, to engage in nonviolent civil disobedience and put myself in the position of being arrested. I also chose, as is my right as an American citizen, not to carry my identification with me.

Organizers of the protest picked this particular intersection to intentionally cut off access to the offices of Joe Arpaio, the Maricopa County Sheriff, who is notorious for his inhumane treatment of suspected illegal immigrants.

As I watch the Phoenix police decked out in riot gear approach, I feel a strange mixture of clarity, resolve, and terror. My chest tightens and I wonder if all my sweating is the result of the relentless Phoenix sun. This is the first time in my thirty-five years as an activist that I am prepared to be arrested for a deliberate act of civil disobedience.

The man who is holding my arm to my left is bigger than I, taller and stouter. His face appears calm despite the fact that his eyebrows are raised as if he is surprised by the intensity of what is happening around him. He is Latino, as is the smaller woman, closer to my size, on my right arm. Angie is her name. I introduced myself a moment ago but didn't have a chance to ask the man's name before we linked arms. His stern expression tells me it's better not to interrupt him now. Angie is wearing a white T-shirt emblazoned with the words "We Will NOT Comply." She wears a wide Mexican bracelet on her wrist, beaded with the colors of the earth and sky—blue, green, orange, and yellow. She watches the police with the eyes of someone who has previously fallen prey to their abuses. I wonder about her story.

My story is that in 2007, I went on a civil rights bus tour of the deep South led by Gordon Gibson, a Unitarian Universalist minister who had spent many years working in Mississippi and who had himself been arrested in Selma, Alabama, in the 1960s, protesting for voting rights for black people. During that tour, I met people who had risked everything for the right to vote. Our group talked with people like Joanne Bland from Selma. As a young child in the early 1960s, Joanne peered longingly into the drugstore window in down-town Selma, craving an ice cream cone, like the ones being enjoyed inside by other little girls her age. She begged her grandmother to let her go in and get one. "No," her grandmother replied sharply, as she pulled her away from the window, "When you get your rights, then you can go in and get ice cream." Joanne joined the civil rights movement that day and, by the time she was thirteen, had been arrested eleven times.

We met with Hollis Watkins, who, in addition to being arrested too many times to count, sang and wrote verses for old spirituals to give courage to those priming themselves for jail. I could imagine Hollis as a strap-ping young teenager with a voice like velvet, embold-ening the other protestors as they nervously gathered outside a church in Jackson, Mississippi, more than forty years ago. He sang,

Ain't gonna let nobody
Turn me 'round,
Turn me 'round,
Turn me 'round,
Ain't gonna let nobody
Turn me 'round,
Keep on a walkin',
Keep on a talkin',
Marchin' up to Freedom Land.

Through their stories and the stories of many other veterans of the civil rights movement, I came to understand, in entirely new ways, the incredible sacrifices that people made for what they believed in.

What had I given up for my beliefs? I had marched for women's rights, for gay and lesbian rights, and against nuclear power. I had protested and leafleted, organized, and made endless phone calls. But what had I really risked? I hadn't chained myself to the White House gate, scaled the fences at the School of the Americas, or thrown blood on the steps of the Pentagon. I hadn't climbed old-growth trees or blocked the entrance to military facilities. I hadn't done anything that would constitute real risk. Truth be told, I viewed the people who did those things as the extremists, the ones who had nothing to lose. I questioned their tactics, the impact that their actions had. How could one person or a small group of people acting outside the law really change anything? But the people I met and the stories I heard about the civil rights movement caused me to question everything I had thought up to this point in my life.

When Fannie Lou Hamer was forty-five years old, she tried to register to vote. Like many African Americans in the fifties and sixties, she was denied her legal right to register. The very next day, the owner of the plantation where she had lived as a sharecropper for seventeen years threw her out of her home—just for *trying* to register.

In the 1960s, two Unitarian Universalists paid the ultimate price at the height of the civil rights movement. James Reeb, a white Unitarian Universalist minister, and two colleagues were taking a shortcut back to Brown Chapel in Selma when three men attacked them with baseball bats. Reeb never regained consciousness and died two days after the attacks. Viola Liuzzo, a white mother of four, a Unitarian Universalist from Detroit, died on the side of a lonely highway as a car pulled up beside her. One of the occupants of that car raised a gun to the open window and shot her in the head. People risked their livelihoods, their safety, their freedom, and their lives to have a stake in this democracy.

I was so moved by the courage, the determination, the ferocity of the stories of the civil rights movement that I helped organize two subsequent bus tours, renamed them pilgrimages, and challenged the pilgrims to evaluate their own spiritual journeys as activists in the context of the movement. The Living Legacy Pilgrimage is now a regular event that attracts people from around the country who want to learn about this extraordinary time in our history. But was that enough? Even with the great amount of time and investment it takes to plan a pilgrimage, it is still what I call "one-off" activism. It's voyeuristic, tidy, sanitary activism. I often hear from participants how transformational the trip was for them and I have to ask, "What has it transformed you *to do?*" Because without action, transformation is an empty bus going nowhere.

For all my words, though, when a call went out from Susan Frederick Gray, a Unitarian Universalist minister based in Phoenix, to UUs across the country to come to Phoenix on May 29, 2010, the day Arizona SB 1070 would be signed into law, I stayed home. Too busy, I said to myself. A few weeks later, another protest was planned for July 29. My friend and colleague, local UU minister Jeanne Pupke, told me she was going and asked me whether I planned to go as well.

"I'm thinking about it," I said, although, quite frankly, until that moment I hadn't really considered it. Knowing Jeanne was going made it a little harder to ignore. I had already missed one opportunity. Now it was pecking at my window again.

I thought about all I had learned about risk from the civil rights movement veterans. I thought about how many times I had asked others about what they were going to do based on what they had learned. I thought about the horrendous abuses that were possible with the enactment of SB 1070, and I began to see this as an opportunity for direct civil disobedience. The police, even Sheriff Joe Arpaio, who calls himself "America's toughest sheriff," cannot require me to carry identification while I'm out on the streets. The proponents say this law does not institutionalize racial profiling. If that's the case, then if I got arrested, with my red hair and fair skin and no identification, would the law be applied equally to me? I suspected not, and consequently, my arrest could point out the obvious hypocrisy.

I thought about that empty bus going nowhere. I thought about all the times I had said no. I tried to imagine how I would face myself in the mirror if I passed up this invitation. I saw an image of myself as a red-headed child cowering in the corner. And then I saw the Selma police hauling the young Joanne Bland off to jail yet again. Which would I be? Would I find the courage to stand up for my beliefs or would I keep pretending I was working for justice? I knew the answer. I could feel it rise up in my body like the blinding sun peeking out from behind dark clouds after a storm. I had to do this if I was going to stay credible, even to myself. I had talked too long. It was time to do something real. I would have to find the courage somewhere. I only hoped I would find it before I got on the plane.

After feeling some resolve in my decision, I poured myself a glass of wine, settled down in my favorite recliner, and flipped on the TV. My partner Wendy would be home soon and I could use a little relaxation before I talked with her about my plans.

It was Saturday night, and instead of the usual news shows, MSNBC's *Lockup* blared from the set. I reached for the remote to find something calmer, but my finger froze in the air as I realized that the show's deep-voiced announcer was describing the Maricopa County Jail, the home of Sheriff Joe Arpaio. Not only is Sheriff Joe the toughest sheriff, the announcer warned, as if speaking directly to me, but his jail is the toughest in America. The jail door slammed hard, the chilling sound of metal against metal echoing down the cold cellblock. The prisoners, covered with tattoos, projected a viciousness that would terrify a ghost on Halloween night. I sat up in my recliner.

The narrator recounted Sheriff Joe's accomplishments. Prisoners are fed only twice a day, and the meals are the cheapest of any jail, only fifteen cents per prisoner. Two thousand prisoners do their time in a tent city, exposed to the searing heat, the desert cold, debilitating dust storms, and torrential thunderstorms. And then there are the chain gangs. Men and — for the first time ever in this country — women and even juveniles are forced to work cleaning up litter, painting over graffiti, and burying the dead. With no coffee, cigarettes, or movies and limited TV, jail time is no picnic — and that, after all, is Sheriff Joe's point.

When the TV show finally ground to an excruciating halt an hour later, I felt as though I had just been run over by that empty bus. Every muscle ached, as I had spent the hour in an acute state of alert. I forced myself to take a few deep breaths and let the tension go. And then I did what I always do: I turned to the Internet to find out more.

I read about how Joe Arpaio routinely orders raids on Hispanic communities, intending to create an atmosphere of fear and terror. I learned that he is being investigated by the federal government for civil rights abuses and has lost multiple lawsuits related to his abuses. I read about his dogged determination to rid his county of anyone who doesn't fit his very narrow definition of a citizen. As all this set in, I thought about the police chiefs from the civil rights movement days, specifically the infamous Jim Clark of Selma and Bull Connor of Birmingham, who used their positions and power to keep people down, to deny them their rights, and to preserve a racially segregated society. I knew my decision to go was correct. It was the only way I could have the right to challenge others to get on the bus. And yet, even after making the decision, I couldn't calm my racing heart or dry my sweaty palms.

When I told Wendy of my plans, I did so with immense trepidation. Ours was a fairly new relationship and I didn't know what she would think of this crazy person who planned to get arrested. Would she reconsider our upcoming wedding? But I knew I had to tell her.

I let her settle into being home for a few minutes, and then took her hand and led her to the sofa. "Hon, can we sit and talk for a minute?" I paused briefly, swallowed hard, and said, "I'm thinking about going to Phoenix and. . . ." A second pause caused her body to stiffen a little; I could feel it in her grip on my hand. With an even harder swallow, I forced out the words, "get arrested."

I let that settle in before I continued. I could see the tension rise in her face. Her eyes grew wide and her mouth rigid, but instead of reacting, she forced herself into a listening posture.

"Tell me more about your decision," she said tightly.

I told her about the mass civil disobedience action that was planned, about Joe Arpaio, and about the thinking that had brought me to my decision. I tried to make it sound safe, easy. *It would be, right?*

"What do you think?" I asked, trying to leave room for her to voice an objection but not sure what I would do with one if I got it.

"I will worry about you," she started slowly, looking down at our clasped hands and then back up at me. "I wish I could go with you but I don't think my school would understand." She looked away again. I wondered if she was fighting back tears. When she started speaking again, I knew she had made up her mind too.

"You have to go," she said. "You have the freedom to go. You have a supportive employer. You have a supportive partner. You have the time and the resources. You have to go. I'm very proud of you." Her eyes glistened and she reached for me. We hugged, deeply and long.

Wendy's response gave me at least a touch of the courage I so desperately sought. I felt my heart slow down a bit and I could breathe a little more deeply. I finally began to believe I might be able to do this, but I wouldn't know until the actual time came.

On July 28, Jeanne and I boarded a plane for Phoenix. I had packed light: sunscreen, pajamas, sunglasses, an extra pair of pants, underwear, socks, a water bottle, and two Standing on the Side of Love T-shirts. What does one pack to go to jail? I didn't have a clue. I hoped I had done all right.

When we arrived at the Phoenix airport, we rented a car and drove directly to the Unitarian Universalist Congregation of Phoenix. Orientation had already begun when we arrived.

As is often my style, I stood for a few minutes in the back and watched, taking in the scene. Seventy-five or so people, ranging in age from what looked to be seventeen to seventy, sat in hard-backed chairs in the Fellowship Hall. A group of about five young adults stood in front, off to the side. I recognized one of them. Betty Jeanne was an experienced activist. She and I had met years earlier at a meeting to organize a group of white antiracists. I suspected she was one of the civil disobedience trainers. Others who I knew, and many who I did not, milled around the perimeter while various Unitarian Universalist leaders spoke.

Dan Furmansky, Standing on the Side of Love campaign manager, said, "This is not just about SB 1070. We are in this for the long haul."

"When we see people pushed to the margins, love and justice are moved to the margins," said Taquiena Boston, director of Multicultural Growth and Witness.

"The legal system is how the powerful oppress those without power. Never doubt the work we are doing is vital," said Peter Morales, president of the Unitarian Universalist Association.

We learned that earlier that afternoon, a federal judge had stayed implementation of several of the more controversial provisions of SB 1070. However, despite the ruling, the protests would go on as planned. Families were still being torn apart. Joe Arpaio was still conducting raids, and in fact, he had promised to start a large-scale operation the very next day to capture undocumented immigrants through traffic violations and bring them to his tent city. Racial profiling was still a fact of life in Arizona.

Okay then, let's get on with it. I was getting impatient as my anxiety about the next day began to get the better of me. I was ready for the talking to be over. I wanted to find out more about this civil disobedience thing and what it would mean for me.

Finally, the speeches wound down and it was time for training. The five young adults, Betty Jeanne among them, took center stage. "We'd like to talk about what civil disobedience is and what it isn't," said the lead trainer. I felt myself taking a deep breath, and scenes from *Lockup* clamored for attention in my head. I tried to quell them but they would not be quieted. This was it. In a few minutes I was going to have to declare publicly that I was willing to engage in civil disobedience or step back and watch as I'd done so many times before.

The question came sooner than I expected: "How many of you plan to participate in CD tomorrow?"

My hand went up before my brain even had time to process the question. I surprised myself with my confidence. When my brain finally caught up, I forced it to match the assurance in my hand. *I have to do this*, I said to myself. Over and over again. *Remember the stories you heard.* I imagined Gordon Gibson, the UU minister who leads the Living Legacy Pilgrimage, getting hauled off to jail in Selma. *Remember the people who risked their lives for justice.* The image of Mrs. Amelia Boynton, the matriarch of the voters' rights movement, bleeding and left for dead on the Edmund Pettus Bridge, flashed in front of my eyes. *Remember the families who are being torn apart by this law.* I recalled the story told by Margaret Regan in *The Death of Josseline* of fourteen-year-old Josseline Quinteros, who died while trying to cross into the United States along the Mexico-Arizona border. *Remember.*

Over the course of the next two hours, the trainers took us through multiple scenarios of what might happen, of what the police might do, of what they might not do. I learned about nonviolent civil disobedience and that it was up to us to decide between nonresistance—

14

going away peacefully—and passive resistance—going limp and being dragged or lifted away. I learned about the intricate planning that goes into a mass civil disobedience action, something that had escaped me before. Liaisons from our group were already working with the police to prevent violence. *Violence?* I could hear a steel door slam in my brain blocking any thoughts of violence from penetrating too deeply. Lawyers were on hand to help when needed. The media had been notified. Everything was in motion.

This time, I was on the bus, and this time, it was going somewhere.

Puente Arizona, a local grassroots migrant and human rights organization, was providing our legal support and would be monitoring the arrests. "Remember to write Puente's number on your arm with a Sharpie so you have it to call them after you get arrested," the trainers instructed.

"Identify a support person who can contact your family members if you are arrested. Make sure they have cell phone and home phone numbers," they told us.

Ah, that makes sense. That's good. Wendy will feel better if she knows, and I'll feel better knowing she knows something. Since Jeanne had to fly back home as soon as the rally ended the next day, I approached Elaine Peresluha, another minister I knew, to be my support person.

She said yes without hesitation. We filled out the paperwork, exchanged phone numbers, and when the training was done, hugged goodnight. Tomorrow was going to be a big day.

Jeanne and I headed back to our hotel for a few hours of rest after stopping at a sporting goods store to pick up a hat. I had forgotten to bring one, and the sun was sounding more menacing with every report.

When we arrived at our hotel room and readied ourselves for the few hours of sleep ahead of us, Jeanne turned to me and asked, "Are you sure about doing this?" I could hear the caring and concern in her voice but was tired of defending my decision, mostly to myself.

I looked her in the eye and responded, maybe a little too sharply. "Yes. Yes, I am."

"You know it will kill me to have to get on a plane if you are sitting in jail." She looked down and away, not willing to engage my stare. "I don't know how to do that."

For the first time, I saw the impact of my decision on the people who loved me. Until that moment, I had been so wrapped up in my decision that I hadn't really considered what their fear must be like. I thought of Wendy back home alone, and I knew that she, that Jeanne, that Elaine, that all the people who loved and supported me were taking risks, too. At that moment, I saw their hands on my shoulders and the dread in their eyes, taking just a bit of the spark out of them. I felt their uneasiness, just as surely as I felt the churning in my own stomach. I also saw their love. I knew they were there for me, and I also knew I couldn't alleviate their fears any more than I could my own.

"Thank you, Jeanne," I said, my voice a lot softer and cracking a little. "I understand. But I have to do this and you have to be back at church. I'll be in good hands. If it happens, there'll be a lot of us in jail together. I'll be okay. And I'll make sure you hear as soon as I get out."

She looked at me, nodded unconvincingly, and with that, we turned out the light. Not surprisingly, sleep did not come easily. I would drift off, only to see the face of one of the men in *Lockup* leering at me and I would wake with a start. I had once heard Eckhart Tolle say you can't think while you are consciously taking deep breaths. I tried to make myself believe him. I forced the air deep into my lungs, past my stomach, and down into my diaphragm. Then I let it slowly escape, pushing out my tension with it. When I finally fell into a shallow and restless sleep, I dreamed of endless running, of frantically looking for something I had lost, of deadlines impossible to meet. I woke achy, unsettled, and queasy.

July 29, 2010, 5:30 a.m. I leave my wallet and all my ID in my suitcase. I already feel a little naked without it but I refuse to second-guess my decision. *Remember the stories,* I remind myself. *Keep yourself focused on those stories.* As Jeanne and I step out into the sunshine, we gaze at a spectacular rainbow that fills the Arizona sky and I soon forget all about ID. Red, orange, yellow, green, blue, indigo, and violet. Room for all under the heavens. I pull out my camera and snap a photo of Jeanne with the rainbow overhead and a copy of the *Arizona Republic* newspaper, displaying the bold headline, "Judge Blocks Heart of Law," in her hands. Whatever happens today, it is going to be a good day.

5:53 a.m. We arrive at Trinity Cathedral for an interfaith worship service to kick off the events of the day. The sanctuary is filling fast as we slide into a pew toward the back. It is already hot. I wipe sweat from my forehead. I look around and I see many UUs I know, some wearing clerical collars, others wearing yellow SSL shirts, some wearing both.

Even earlier this morning, a group of people representing many faiths, Latinos/Latinas/Hispanics and whites, women and men, young and old, who had been sitting vigil at the Federal Courthouse from the day SB 1070 was passed until the day it was enacted—102 days in total—had processed from the courthouse to the cathedral. They are seated in the front rows.

As the worship service begins, we hear the stories of resistance from those who sat vigil. I add them to the other stories already in my head. A woman mourns her husband, taken by immigration authorities. She doesn't know where he is. Another cries for the teenage son she hasn't heard from since he tried to cross the border. A man tells of being arrested and beaten, only to be released when it was discovered that he is an American citizen. We hear prayers and inspiration from Christian, Jewish, Muslim, and Unitarian Universalist faith leaders. *Spirit of life and love, watch over these people today as they stand for justice. Give them the courage of the prophets. Guide them as they resist those who dishonor the humanity of all your people.*

And we sing—the same hymns that Hollis Watkins sang in the civil rights movement so many years ago:

Ain't gonna let nobody
Turn me 'round,
Turn me 'round,
Turn me 'round.

As we sing the verses "Ain't gonna let no jailhouse turn me 'round," and "Ain't gonna let Joe Arpaio turn me 'round," I remember Hollis telling us how he survived in the harshest jail conditions by remembering to sing. I feel his spirit fill me with a fire that makes even the Phoenix heat feel cool.

7:59 *a.m.* The service ends with a robust, spirit-filled performance of "We Shall Overcome," and we file out of the cathedral and into the streets. A woman with deep brown skin, a high forehead suggestive of a Mayan heritage, a long white T-shirt, and a yellow bandana wrapped like a sweatband around her head stands silently on the street corner across from the church, a look of quiet determination on her face. She holds a simple black and white sign adorned with the Statue of Liberty and the words ASK ME 4 MY PAPERS. I nod to her as I pass. She nods back but never changes her resolute expression.

Another woman, younger than the first, with straight, shoulder-length brown hair, stands unmoving in the hot morning sun, her legs pressed together tightly like a molded statue in the town square. The sign she holds, more colorful than the first, shows a woman in a bright yellow shirt against a red background holding yet another sign high above her head. That sign reads UNDOCUMENTED UNAFRAID, and in smaller letters NO TENEMOS MIEDO (We have no fear). What courage it takes for these women to publicly declare their status, to challenge law enforcement to arrest them, on this day of all days. I see the pain dripping from their eyes, the courage bursting from their chests, the determination set in their feet, and I feel more certain with each step I take.

9:30 *a.m.* Three and a half hours into the day. The sun is almost directly overhead already, and its rays beat down on us as though they were being reflected through a magnifying glass. We are in Cesar Chavez Plaza directly across from the Wells Fargo Building where Sheriff Joe Arpaio has his office. It is ironic that Cesar Chavez, the Mexican American known for his nonviolent advocacy of human rights, and Joe Arpaio, known for his violent disregard of those same rights, should face each other in this place. It seems a fitting spot for a showdown. Organizers ask those who are planning to engage in civil disobedience and their supporters to go to an area toward the back of the park for further instructions. Marching and speeches are over. It is time for action.

The police presence is strong. Numerous police vehicles, vans, SUVs, and cars are parked at every visible intersection. Officers, dressed in black uniforms, gather in groups in front of the vehicles. Others form a line—three rows deep—dissecting the street midway down the block. Still others form barriers between the crowds on the sidewalk and the street. They all wear helmets with face guards, so it's impossible to see any expression on their faces. Some wear long-sleeve shirts and even black gloves so no part of their skin is visible. *How can they stand the heat? Are they even human or are they robots programmed to do Joe Arpaio's bidding?* Then I remember that these are Phoenix City Police. They are not sheriff's deputies. *Will that make a difference?* Other city police officers wear short sleeves, showing their arms and hands, which gives me a slight degree of comfort—at least I can see that they are human.

As I approach the group at the back of the plaza, I notice people passing around black Sharpies and am reminded to write Puente's phone number on my arm. I spot my support person, Elaine, and greet her with a hug. She inscribes the number in big, bold print on my right forearm. The number marks me in some way I cannot explain and I feel unsettled by it. Though I know there is no comparison, I can't help but think about the arms of German concentration camp victims. I try to shake off the feeling.

"You are going to be blocking the intersection to prevent Sheriff Joe from entering or leaving his office. A group of local protestors will be blocking the other end of the street," the lead organizer, the same young man who led the training the previous night, explains.

This is the first time we know exactly what action we'll be engaged in. I imagine us standing firm in a tight circle, arms interlocked, chanting or singing together, facing the lines of police waiting for us—waiting for them. My pulse quickens, but being able to imagine it helps my shoulders to relax a little.

"In all likelihood," he shouts so he can be heard above the din of the other protestors on the other side of the plaza, "the police will give three warnings before they arrest you. That's not guaranteed though, so be ready."

What does that mean exactly? Ready for what? Ready to run, ready to sit down, ready to put my hands up?

"The pavement is very hot and it will burn you, so if you choose to sit down, don't do it without something under you. The support people will have mats to give you if you want to sit down. They'll also have water. It's important to drink, to stay hydrated. We don't want anyone passing out from the heat. So be sure to ask for water.

"At the beginning, you'll be facing each other, holding a banner. At some point, probably after the first warning, we'll ask you to drop the banner, turn around, and link arms. Like this." He demonstrates linking arms with two people near him. "At that point you'll be facing the police. That's when it might get scarier. Try to find someone you know in the crowd. Look at them. If you change your mind and decide not to get arrested, that's the time to leave the circle. There is no shame in that. Just do what you need to do. If you stay, chances are high you will be arrested."

We practice standing with our elbows linked with the elbows on either side of us. I imagine the line of police moving toward us. I squeeze my biceps tighter and feel the sweat of my partner's arm against mine. *Remember why you are doing this. Remember the families being torn about by this law, by Joe Arpaio's actions. Remember the woman who lost her son. Remember the missing husband. Remember.* We practice finding our support person's face. I find Elaine in the crowd. She smiles and nods her head in encouragement. I clench my fist, release it, and make myself breathe.

"You should decide now what you will do when the police move to arrest you," the organizer says. "If you want to go willingly, drop your arms and move out of the circle."

We practice dropping our arms and feel the circle tightening behind us, excluding us, like in a game of musical chairs. But this is no game.

"If you want to resist, drop your arms and go limp when the officer grabs you. You might fall, so be ready for that." We talk together briefly and agree—we will all go willingly.

"You ready?" the leader asks.

"Yes," we shout as if we're about to run out from the locker room to the cheering fans at a football game. We're as ready as we'll ever be. And so, the procession begins.

Under the searing sun, we march through Cesar Chavez Plaza. I hear someone on a megaphone calling a chant. "Hey, hey, ho, ho, Sheriff Joe has got to go." We walk past him without joining in, our thoughts totally engrossed in the task ahead. I see a television news reporter interviewing one of the march leaders. We walk by unnoticed. I suspect that soon their cameras will be turned on us. We march down the sidewalk and into the intersection. The police stand with their hands on their shiny black belts—at the ready. I walk to the far side of the street and stop at the edge of the large banner that is already laid out for us on the pavement. HUMAN RIGHTS ZONE, it proclaims in big block letters.

10:22 a.m. As though I'm signaled to do so, I bend to pick up the edge of the banner. As I stand up, I look around at the faces of the thirty or so other people holding the banner with me. No one looks panicked, but some are clenching their teeth, their jaws tight and their cheeks drawn. Most are wearing Standing on the Side of Love shirts like mine, but the man and woman on either side of me are not. I assume they are local folks. I don't know them but I still feel a strong bond with them. *Estamos en la lucha juntos. We are in the struggle together.*

We are now blocking the intersection, although with all the police vehicles parked at every corner, we aren't actually stopping any traffic. They have already done that. We chant, "Human rights now" and "Hey, hey, ho, ho, Sheriff Joe has got to go," but mostly we stand there waiting, watching. For some reason, an expression of my father's comes to mind as I try to keep down the bile that forms in my throat: "My mouth tastes like the inside of a motorman's glove," he'd say. I never knew what a motorman's glove tasted like but I imagine this is it. The old, dirty leather sticks at the back of

25

my mouth. I smell the sweat, the oil, the exhaust. I try not to choke. Someone offers me a bottle of water. I take it and drink greedily, letting it wash the leather out of my mouth.

10:37 a.m. From the corner of my eye I see something move like a line of dancers approaching the front of the stage. I look to my left to see the column of police advance toward us. I turn to my right. That line is moving too. I hear a whooshing sound as the blood rushes to my head and feel my pulse pound against my neck. I strain to hear Hollis's voice singing in my ear.

Ain't gonna let nobody
Turn me 'round,
Turn me 'round
Turn me 'round

The song fades too quickly. I try to retrieve it, but all I hear is "turn me 'round, turn me 'round," like a scratched record. No other words come to mind.

10:51 a.m. Our organizers tell us to drop the banner, turn around, and link arms. *Has there been a warning by the police? I didn't hear it,* I think, but I do as they ask. The circle is smaller now as we move closer to each other in order to link our arms together. I am standing on the black and white banner just below the large block letters spelling the word RIGHTS. I smell the sweat of the people I'm connected to. It smells like earth, and hard work, and love.

I look into the crowd on the sidewalk and spot Jeanne. She sees me too and smiles a worried smile. "I'm okay," I mouth to her, trying to give her a reassuring nod. She snaps my picture. Knowing she is there, documenting this for me, helps to settle some of the intensifying queasiness in my stomach.

11:00 a.m. A Latino man with a large video camera on his shoulder, the kind the professional media use, approaches me. I expect him to ask me a question, but instead he steps up close to my face. I feel his warm breath on my neck. He leans directly into my ear and whispers, "Thank you." Tears well up in my eyes. As he steps back, I look at him. His eyes are soft but enveloped in a sea of turmoil.

I smile and mutter, *"De nada."* You're welcome. I'm sure he doesn't know it but he has restored my faltering courage. My tears mix with sweat and I realize I can't wipe my face without unlinking my arms. I let the tears run down my cheeks, and I feel cleansed, baptized into this community of people fighting for their lives.

A police officer, the first one I've seen without a helmet, has a small amplifier in his left hand and a microphone in his right. He approaches the crowd in the street. "Members of the media," he says in a loud, forceful voice suggestive of a Marine drill sergeant commanding his troops. "Members of the media, if you do not clear the intersection, you will be subject to arrest. Members of the media, if you do not clear the intersection, you will be subject to arrest."

That, I fear, is our second warning. Our organizers tell everyone, all our supporters, and all those who are linking arms with me, "Now is the time to move to the sidewalk if you don't want to be arrested. Get back on the sidewalk if you don't want to risk arrest." The supporters move back, but the circle feels firm.

The third warning comes quickly after that. Several police officers walk around us and say in normal conversational voices, "If you stay on the street, you will be arrested. You need to get back on the sidewalk if you want to avoid arrest." I hear someone respond back to them, in a voice that reminds me of the insistent but gentle tide rolling up on the beach, "Thank you, officer, but we are staying here."

11:13 a.m. A police officer steps in front of me. He is tall and looms over me. I feel his hot breath on my face—like the photographer's but different. He says, "Please come with me. You are under arrest."

I am surprised by the caring tone of his voice. He sounds as if he's offering to help me out of a car, not take me to jail. He takes my right arm. I feel the protective arms of the other protestors drop away from me as he guides me, like a jockey leading a horse, out of the circle and to the other side of the street. As we walk, I feel a shadow pass over the sun, darkening the day. I look up to see a cloudless sky and I wonder whose spirit might have floated by, offering me courage.

I see members of our clergy sitting with their arms linked on the hot pavement. *I hope they're sitting on mats*, I think, as I imagine a mass of hot tar burning their tender skin. When we reach a large police van, the officer stops and asks me to put my hands behind my back. As I slip them behind me, my hands become the hands of every criminal on every detective show I have ever watched. And just like on TV, he snaps hot metal handcuffs on my wrists. They are on too tight and pinch the skin at the base of my hands. I look up and am relieved to see Elaine pacing back and forth on the sidewalk talking on her cell phone. "I'm calling Wendy," she shouts at me. "Thanks," I holler back.

As I wait for more instructions from the gentlemanly officer, another officer approaches, directing an older African-American woman, probably in her early sixties, to stand by me. I don't know her but since she is wearing an SSL shirt, I suspect she is a Unitarian Universalist. I see the distress in her flushed face. "I just need to sit down for a moment," she says, looking around frantically. "Is there any place I can sit down?"

The officer tells her no but if she wants to go over to the EMS vehicle she can do that. Then he says, "Listen, it doesn't get easier from here. In fact, it'll get a lot harder. You have to decide if you really want to be arrested. If you don't, I'll let you go right now."

Decide if you want to be arrested? I thought that opportunity passed with the third warning and the hand on my arm. But here he was giving this woman who was clearly overcome by the heat one more chance. I wonder if Sheriff Joe's deputies would be so kind. The city police appear to be cut from a different cloth.

"Thank you, officer," she says, "but a lot of people went to jail for me to have my rights, so I could be here today. Now, it's my turn to pay them back. I intend to go through with this."

I smile when I hear her words—words I have said to myself many times over the past few days. People in the civil rights movement went to jail to secure voting rights for African Americans; women, such as Alice Paul and Lucy Burns, went to jail in the women's suffrage movement for my rights. The stories come flooding back once again. I see the resolute faces of the women I passed outside the church this morning. I hear the sobs of children whose parents have been snatched up in a workplace raid. I see the grateful eyes of the tormented photographer who whispered in my ear a few minutes ago. I imagine the fear and determination pulsing in the veins of the people who plan to cross the border tonight, seeking a better life. I see Joanne Bland and Hollis Watkins, James Reeb and Viola Liuzzo, and the chorus of intrepid men and women who paved the way in another place, in another time. I imagine them encircling me, cheering me on. I hear them singing songs of the civil rights movement to augment my resolve, and I know I am ready to do what needs to be done.

The arresting officer, a tall, thin white man, tips the mask of his riot helmet upward to reveal a kind, almost baby face. He reaches behind me and unlocks the handcuffs placed there only moments before. "Put your hands together in front of you," he directs. I do as he says. He repositions the cuffs around my wrists and snaps them shut again, my thumbs pressed together, palms facing each other. This is a little more comfortable and gives me more flexibility.

"Put your rings, necklace, and any other jewelry into the bag," he instructs me.

I awkwardly remove my gold ring and drop it into the plastic bag he holds open in front of me. I struggle to take off my necklace with handcuffs around my wrists, especially with the chain stuck to my sweat-drenched skin. But I manage, resecure its latch, and drop it into the bag.

"What about your pockets? Empty those too. And your buttons, take those off," he continues.

I unpin my "No human is illegal" and "Standing on the Side of Love" buttons from my bright yellow Standing on the Side of Love T-shirt. I take off my sunglasses and my watch. I remove my cherished iPhone from the waistband of my pants. I extract the small purple notebook from my back pocket. From my belt loop, I unhook the blue, soft-sided, Detroit Zoo sunglasses case containing a pen, a USB thumb drive, and a Clarendon hotel key card. Everything goes into the bag.

Without the things that adorn my body, that identify me directly or indirectly, I feel naked. I am now anonymous, unidentified, and unidentifiable. I am nobody. Anybody. I can prove nothing about my identity, just like every person taken into custody without proof of immigration status. It is now my word against theirs. Only one thing separates us. My white skin automatically affords me more trust. Or, at least, so I hope.

The officer grabs my arm a little more roughly this time and directs me to step into the waiting van. As I step up, I look back over my shoulder and see Elaine standing there. She is still holding the phone to her ear. I nod to her and she nods backs. I am reassured, knowing she is describing to Wendy exactly what is happening. I hope Wendy feels the same.

The van is dark, and it takes a minute for my eyes to adjust from the bright sun outside. I take a seat on a bench that runs lengthwise along the side of the van. I greet the two women who are already there. "Hi, how're you doing?" I say, not really expecting an answer.

They nod. We sit in silence, and wait. The van's motor is running, so it is cool inside, a moment's relief from the heat. One by one, more women enter the van. The remaining seats are soon filled, but we still sit there.

Eventually, the occupants of the van start talking, and soon they are chattering away as if they are waiting in line for a Disney attraction. When I feel anxious, I go quiet, turn inward to myself. For others, I guess, it's just the opposite. I only know I want to stay alert, careful, attentive to everything happening around me. I know that even though my white privilege will carry me through a lot of things, situations like this can go terribly wrong. I prepare myself to be always watchful.

When the van finally starts to move, my heart jumps. *Where will they take us? Are we really going to Sheriff Arpaio's jail? Maybe they'll just take us to a holding area and then release us. Maybe. . . .*

I don't wonder long, however. Within a few short blocks, I see a sign across a large garage-type door:

Maricopa County Jail
Sheriff Joe Arpaio

The door opens and the van enters the abyss.

STORMTROOPERS

———◆———

We enter a cavernous space that encompasses half of the first floor of the Maricopa County Jail building. The van makes a tight U-turn and parks. A deputy strides up to the back door of the van, jerks it open, and orders us to remain inside. "We're on lockdown," he barks, as if that explained everything. "Stay here until you are directed otherwise."

Lockdown? What does that mean? Has there been a bomb threat? A terrorist attack? Or is this somehow related to us? I strain to see outside the narrow van windows and open door. As I take in the scene unfolding around us, my state of alert escalates from orange to red.

On all three visible sides of the van, squadrons of police gather in various degrees of orderliness. One group, dressed in green pants, khaki short-sleeved shirts, helmets, and black bulletproof vests, stands two abreast at full attention listening to orders shouted at them by their commander. Another group, notable for their lack of riot gear, gathers in loose formation. Some chat one-on-one and others stand quietly by. My breath catches when I see members of a third squadron start jumping up and down. They are making grunting sounds and pumping their arms in the air. Some clutch short shotguns with wide barrels to their chests. *Those must be tear gas guns.* Others hold large clear shields with the word "Sheriff" in big white letters printed across the front. All are wearing helmets with the face shields down. The image of the imperial stormtroopers of *Star Wars* comes to mind. My mind starts reeling. The stormtroopers' main mission is to put down insurrection and establish imperial authority. *Is that what's going on here? Is Joe Arpaio establishing his authority?*

The air is charged like a summer storm blowing ominously in our direction, but instead of thunder, I hear chanting. Suddenly, the pieces fall into place.

Last night, I heard that organizers were planning a second, much more secretive civil disobedience action to run concurrently with ours. I also heard that it involved higher profile folks: Peter Morales, the president of the Unitarian Universalist Association; Susan Frederick-Gray, the minister from one of the local Phoenix congregations; and Salvador Reza, a civil rights leader from Puente Arizona. In all likelihood, those people and others have barricaded the jail's main vehicle entrance, the one that the squadrons of officers now face. If I am correct, then any minute, the sheriff's deputies will open that big door and the stormtroopers will engage the protestors.

"Hey, everybody," I shout, in a voice so imperious, it startles even me. Its sharpness severs their conversations in midsentence. "Do you know what they are about to do?" I lean forward so I can engage the eyes of as many in the van as possible. "Our people are on the other side of that door." I point wildly at the garage door. "Do you hear them?" Ears turn toward the sounds coming from the other side of that oversized garage door.

"What do you want?" a voice bellows through a megaphone.

"Justice," we hear a crowd shout in response.

"When do you want it?"

"Now!"

Although I can't make out all the words, I know the rhythm of the chant; it was one we chanted—out there, on the street. Those of us in the van draw a communal breath as the realization of what is about to happen hits us all.

"When the police open that door," I continue, "and send these troops out there, all hell could break loose. This could be bad." I shake my head and suck in air to catch my breath. "Very bad."

Almost as if on cue, the large four-panel door separating us from the protestors splits open. It creaks and groans as the opening grows larger and larger. We watch as if the curtain on an immense stage is being drawn back for the final climactic scene. The oppressive midday heat rushes in and assaults us in the cool van. I crane my neck to get a better view. At least several hundred people are swarming outside the door. With fists raised high over their heads, some shout, "Power to the people! Power to the people!" Others chant indistinguishably in the cacophony around them, but their sentiment—anger and resolve—is clear.

The lines of police advance. First, the sheriff's deputies with helmets, bulletproof vests, and tear-gas guns press forward. Then a line of police holding shields form a barrier to keep the protestors from rushing in.

"Boo! Boo!" come the shouts from the throng, as two deputies lead Peter Morales into the building. His yellow Standing on the Side of Love shirt and white fedora stand in stark contrast to the black uniforms and helmets of the deputies. When we see Peter, a spontaneous cheer goes up from us in the van. "Yay!" we holler as loudly as we can. He looks in our direction and smiles, which causes us to yell even more stridently, "Yay! Go, Peter! Alright!" We stomp our feet and the van starts to shake. Several deputies look in our direction. They are not smiling.

Salvador Reza, in his blood-red "Legalize Arizona" T-shirt, follows soon after; we cheer a second time, "Yay, Sal!" The sight of these two leaders getting arrested emboldens our sense of defiance. "We're with you! Thank you!" we scream, hoping he can hear us.

At that, a deputy storms over to the van and slams the van door shut on us. The force of his action thrusts us back against our seats. "Quiet down in there," he commands. We can see only a part of his face but his message is clear. They mean business, and one misstep on any of our parts could put us all in danger. The weight of what we are witnessing settles into my chest as surely as if a concrete block has been thrown against it.

With the van door closed and the mass of deputies pressing forward into the crowd, we stretch even more to take in the scene unfolding in front of us.

"Arrest Arpaio! Not the people. Arrest Arpaio! Not the people."

The crowd's strident chanting, although muffled, pulsates through the van and through us. A group of deputies, unencumbered by riot gear, crosses in front of the line of shields and approaches the crowd. I see them drag a group of five or six protestors through the door and into the building, dropping them unceremoniously on the floor. I try to make sense of the jumble of bodies as they struggle to right themselves on the floor. Their forearms extend through long sections of yellow PVC pipe, joining one to another, to form a human barrier. The words "NO 1070" are painted in big red letters on the pipe. Even under arrest, the protestors, Rev. Susan Frederick-Gray among them, remain staunchly attached.

A deputy approaches them. *What is he holding?* I strain to make out what he has gripped in his hands. Then I see it. It is a large circular saw. I feel like a rag has been stuffed down my throat, and I choke. I know this type of saw and understand its vicious power. The deputy pulls the cord on the saw and it comes alive with a roar. An image of the saw severing the PVC pipe quickly forms in my mind. I imagine the pungent odor of burning plastic as it bores through the pipe. As the saw goes deeper, I see blood spurting out in all directions, slicing their arms apart. I imagine their cries of anguish.

Oh, please don't hurt them.

At that moment, the van door flies open. "Get out of the van," a burly deputy with a buzz cut commands. "Line up against the wall." His menacing voice penetrates the nightmare forming in my mind. I shake my head to vanquish the ghastly images.

Since I can't use my handcuffed hands to brace myself, I step carefully out of the van so as not to tumble onto the hard concrete floor. We shuffle single file in the direction he points. I can still hear the buzzing of the saw, but I can no longer see the tangle of conjoined protestors. They are obscured by lines of stormtroopers waiting to be called into action. My time as a spectator is over. I now must focus my attention on my own piece in this drama. I am about to become an inmate in the Maricopa County Jail.

JAIL

———◆———

If I could describe the jail experience in one word, it would be *dehumanizing*. Everything and everyone in the jail conspires to degrade and debase the inmates— physically, mentally, and emotionally. After my time in the Maricopa County Jail, the more cynical side of me has come to believe that this is one way the guards, under the auspices of the sheriff, can mete out their own punishment to those they incarcerate. I can't explain why the guards feel the need to punish. Or maybe the truth is that I'm afraid to explain it because if I do, it would be harder for me to believe in the inherent worth and dignity of every person. All I can do is describe what I witnessed and leave the analysis to you, the reader, to come up with your own explanations.

It began even before I was booked. Handcuffs still tight around my wrists, a deputy directed me to a private cell in the booking area. She handed me a large plastic urine cup, shoved me inside, and snarled, "We need a urine sample. Pee in the cup." The metal door banged shut behind me.

Finding some moxie from the absurdity of the situation, I yelled back to her, "How can I do that with handcuffs on? Can you take these off?"

"No," she snapped back. "Those are the city's. I don't have the keys. Deal with it."

Phoenix City Police had arrested me. She was a Maricopa County Sheriff's Deputy. Cooperation was apparently not their strong suit.

I stood there in stunned silence. The stillness of the eight-by-eight-foot concrete hole enveloped me. For the first time, I was alone in a jail cell, my hands locked in front of me, the door locked behind me. The air smelled musty and stagnant. I fought back tears—tears that threatened to expose my fear. If I was to get through this intact, I could not afford either. I turned instead to the task at hand.

I reviewed her directive in my head. She's expecting me to take my pants down, hold a cup under me, pee into it, pull my pants back up, and re-zip and re-button them, all while my wrists are cuffed tightly together—and I'm supposed to do this without spilling the contents of the cup? Where is Houdini when I need him?

I suppose I could have set the cup on the floor, but I never thought to do that. Instead, I fumbled with the button on my khakis with my right hand while I tried to maintain a hold on the cup with my left. When I succeeded in opening the button, I pulled the zipper down as far as I could. Then, I twisted and squirmed to peel my khakis off my sticky, sweat-covered skin. When they finally fell to the floor, I wondered if I would ever get them back on again.

I will skip over the details of what came next, except to say that when the deputy returned, I handed her a cup filled with and *covered in* my urine. She collected it in her ungloved hands. Although I felt a sense of pleasure in leaving Sheriff Joe a puddle of my urine on his floor, my pants carried the stench of sweat, mixed with equal parts urine and humiliation.

Absorbed in wondering how offensive my stench might be, I sat on a long bench with other arrestees, waiting to be booked. But the room around me bustled with activity and I soon lost my self-focus. A high counter separated us from three or four deputies plugging away at computers. Several deputies scurried around with papers and folders in their hands, a few stood behind the counter conferring with each other in groups of two or three, while others escorted arrestees into and out of the area. An older white-haired woman wearing a Standing on the Side of Love t-shirt sat across a desk from a female deputy. The deputy never looked up from her keyboard as she, in an almost machine-like voice, peppered the woman with questions: "Name," "Address," "Date of birth." A man with tattoos covering every bit of his visible skin and shaved head stood against the wall, while a deputy snapped a photo of him. His mug shot, I suppose.

It was then I came face to face with the brutality of Joe Arpaio's force. A young man with shiny black hair and a dark complexion sat on the bench two seats down from me. Blood stained his "No human is illegal" T-shirt. His eye was swollen shut. Cuts and blotches marred his right cheek and chin. I leaned toward him and asked, "You OK?"

"Yeah," he said. "I wasn't even planning to get arrested. A couple deputies just dragged me to the side of the building and starting punching me." He looked down at the floor. "I didn't do anything." I could hear the bitterness in his voice, but it was bitterness imbued with sadness.

"I'm sorry," I said. I looked down at the floor with him. What else was there to say?

If I regret anything in this whole experience, it is what I did soon after I encountered this man—a man who had been beaten, in all likelihood, because he fit someone's profile of an undocumented immigrant. I had chosen not to carry my ID that day to stand in solidarity with people like him. Yet when the booking officer asked, "Place of birth?" I answered without a second thought, "Ann Arbor, Michigan." As soon as it was out of my mouth, I knew I had blown it. I should have said, "a hospital," or "I don't know," but instead, in that rote response I've given so many times before, I claimed my United States citizenship and confirmed what I'm sure they already assumed. They had profiled me too, and I made it easy for them to validate their profile.

After booking, a deputy directed me through a doorway labeled "Acceptance," an ironic name for the entrance to the inner sanctum of Joe Arpaio's jail. "Take off your shoes," a deputy waiting on the other side directed. "And take out your shoelaces and put them in that bin. You'll get those back when you're released."

I did as I was told. Except for losing my shoelaces, the rest of their search was no more invasive than a TSA pat-down. I'm not sure what that says about the TSA.

When a deputy finally led me to a holding cell and slammed the metal and glass door behind me, I joined a number of other protestors, distinguished mostly by the sayings on their T-shirts, and a few other inmates— probably twenty in all.

I gingerly stepped over three women sleeping on the floor, their bodies curled up tightly as if protecting themselves from unknown attackers. When I made it to the other side of the cell, I propped myself against the wall opposite the door. I looked around to assess my surroundings and determine my place in this new environment.

I counted the concrete blocks that made up the cell and estimated its size to be 336 square feet (14 by 24), including an area partitioned off to partially conceal a toilet. That gave us each about seventeen square feet— roughly three feet by five feet. Not nearly enough room for everyone to lie down if we chose to. Barely enough room to sit.

The three-foot wall that separated the toilet from the rest of the room offered little privacy and certainly no protection from the odors that emanated from it. If we wanted a little more privacy, we pulled the thirty-gallon plastic trash can in front of us as we squatted on the toilet. When we flushed, a stream of water flowed out from the top of the tank to refill it. From this we could wash our hands or, if we dared, fill a water bottle. The stream also splattered the top of the toilet seat in a futile effort to clean it. This disgusted me more than anything else in the cell. Nobody wants a wet toilet seat, so it forced each of us to wipe the seat before using the toilet. I hated even imagining the jail cell design meeting in which this was proposed.

A concrete bench extended around a portion of the cell wall, creating a limited amount of seating. A metal divider protruded from the bench every two and a half feet or so—yet another intentional design, this one to prevent us from lying down on the bench.

The three phones on the wall caught me by surprise. The cells I've seen on TV never had phones. No one, at any point, had asked me if I wanted to make a call. I guess this was why. The phones could be used at any time, by anyone in the cell—but collect calls only, which meant no calls to cell phones. When one of the phones became available, I maneuvered my way over to it.

Our trainers had instructed us to write our attorneys' numbers in permanent marker on our arms. *But what about personal numbers? Who memorizes phone numbers these days?* I hoped I could remember Wendy's home phone number.

One ring. Two rings. Four rings. I had a sinking feeling in my stomach. What if I had the number wrong? Then I heard her voice, "We're not home right now. Please leave a message."

We're not home right now? I'm sitting in jail and you're not home? Where the hell are you? My annoyance quickly morphed into disappointment. I left a message: "I'm okay. I'll try you back later." I knew talking with her would have grounded me, but I would have to find ways to ground myself.

I had no idea what time it was when I tried to call Wendy. I've worn a watch since I was seven years old — not finding it on my wrist when I instinctively looked down at it unmoored me. Time lost all meaning, and yet time meant everything to me. I searched for any discernible markers to keep me anchored.

"The City Court closes at five so you'll be out of here by then," one of the friendlier guards said when she deposited another prisoner into our cell. We had been arrested around noon and I figured that by the time we got to our cells, it had to be after two.

Each time a guard opened the cell door, I expected

her to call my name to go to court. It would be any time now, I was certain of it. Until, that is, a guard announced, with a little more satisfaction in her voice than I would have liked, "You might as well get comfortable. Looks like you'll be spending the night. City Court is closed for the day. It doesn't open again until ten tomorrow morning."

Her words hit me with the same force with which she slammed shut the cell door. *Spending the night? Without being arraigned? We're not getting out?* All those stories from civil rights movement days when people rotted in jail for weeks or even months flooded my brain. I forced myself to banish them from my head. Instead, I made myself focus on how I was going to change my airline reservation. That seemed much easier to worry about.

Everybody seemed to take the news amazingly well. But with the knowledge that a minimum of fifteen hours loomed ahead of us, discovering the actual time became a treasure hunt. The unyielding glare of the florescent lights created an endless day that did not ease into dusk, did not fade into the comforting darkness, did not greet us with the new morning light. This day tortured us with its interminable brightness. Without time, the day loses its frame, and with it goes our sense of self. Discovering the time, being able to calculate how long we had been in the confines of this place and how long until we could hope to be out again, restored some stability and kept disorientation at bay.

From each new arrival to our cell, we'd greedily demand, "What time were you arrested? Was it dark yet? What time do you last remember? How long did your processing take?" With each answer, we'd piece together our own invisible clock, marked by vagaries and supposition rather than minute and hour hands. Each time we felt confident we had narrowed it down, we'd smile knowingly at each other as if we had stolen something back from our jailers, something they conspired to keep from us.

One of the more experienced inmates, a young African-American woman, probably in her late twenties, with short-cropped hair and an indistinguishable tattoo on the right side of her neck, sensed our need to find markers to help us gauge the time. "They feed us twice a day, 6 p.m. and 6:30 a.m.," she said. "That's a good way to figure out what time it is."

However, with the mention of food, time became less significant. I was hungry. We had arrived in Phoenix almost twenty-four hours before. I had nibbled a bit at the potluck they had for us when we arrived at the church, but I had been too hyped up to eat much. Then when we got going that morning, it was much too early to eat. At lunch time, we were out on the street in the midst of our protest. So despite my disappointment about having to stay in jail overnight, I looked forward to some food. Until I got it.

When the food cart arrived, I assume at around 6 p.m., a guard handed each inmate a clear plastic bag.

I remembered learning in that MSNBC *Lockup* episode that Sheriff Joe spends fifteen cents per prisoner for each meal. I secured an open spot on the concrete bench to examine what seven and a half cents could buy. I reached my hand into the bag and extracted two six-inch wheat buns, an ounce-sized plastic container of smooth peanut butter, two oranges, a package of six broken sandwich cookies, an eight-ounce plastic bottle of red "juice," a napkin, and a plastic knife.

"Get used to it," one woman said from across the cell. "We get the same shit twice a day, every day."

"Every meal?" I shot back, incredulous.

"Every meal here," she said. "If you get transferred to Estrella or Tent City (two other jails where women are incarcerated), you get this shit for breakfast and then some other shit in a Styrofoam container for dinner. Some kinda meat shit and some overcooked vegetables. I'd rather have this. At least you know what it is."

I loaded a bun with peanut butter and took my first bite. The peanut butter stuck to the roof of my mouth and the bread stuck with it. I chewed painstakingly and finally swallowed it. The bread was not as bad as I thought it would be. In other circumstances, I might actually have enjoyed it. Then again, maybe I was just hungry.

I was surprised to feel full before finishing it all. I carefully wrapped my leftovers—one orange, the crumbled cookies, and a couple of bites of bread—in the plastic bag for later. I didn't know then that I would not get that opportunity.

After the guards decided that we'd had adequate time for our meal, they opened the huge metal and glass cell door and ordered us to line up in the hall. A jail trusty, dressed in the standard striped jumpsuit, pink socks, pink sandals, and pink underwear (we didn't see his underwear, but we had heard about Sheriff Joe-issued uniforms) docilely slid into the cell, mop and bucket in his hands, head down, eyes averted from ours, and mopped the cell. He threw any food left in the cell into the trash, including my carefully wrapped bag of leftovers, and replaced the trash bag with a fresh one. As if she could hear the complaint rising up into my throat, the guard said sharply, "Don't want roaches."

Or for us to have a snack during the twelve-and-a-half-hour stretch between meals. Can't have that.

After dinner, we had nothing to do but wait. Some women talked, others told jokes, and some tried to find a way to sleep. All I could do was try to get warm. I've lived in cold weather, but the cold inside the jail chilled me more deeply than any I had ever felt. It invaded my bloodstream like venom, quickly and methodically annihilating any warmth I still possessed from the Phoenix midday sun. All my thoughts converged on the single obsession of finding or generating heat. I tried to imagine the 104-degree temperature on the street that morning, to trick my brain into believing the sun was still beating down on me. I rubbed my bare arms. I held them close against my body. I even mimicked the more experienced inmates, who pulled their arms out of their shirts sleeves and hugged themselves tightly under their clothes. But I quickly discovered I didn't like that feeling—like a straightjacket holding down the flailing arms of an unruly mental patient—and I pulled my arms back out again. When we complained to our jailers about the cold, they said the temperature was set low to ward off the spread of disease. Or was it kept low in order to spread dis-ease?

Dehumanizing people takes many forms. It might start with physical discomfort, humiliation, and disorientation, but eventually, it becomes verbal. The guards took great pleasure in calling us "the yellow-shirts," a reference to the Standing on the Side of Love T-shirts we wore. Seeing several of the women lying on the cell floor trying to get some rest, one of the guards said, "What do you call a white person between two yellow shirts?" Without waiting for an answer, he replied, "A Twinkie, of course." But his laughter turned quickly to spite. "You're all Twinkies. You think you can come in here and change anything?" His hostility rolled up from the center of his being and spewed from his mouth. "Go with all your Mexican friends back to where you came from."

Another shouted at us, "If I was the judge, I'd set bail at five hundred thousand dollars each and say 'protest that, you morons.'"

I crossed my arms in front of me for protection. I found myself struggling to hang on to my commitment to nonviolence and to ascribe to him, or to any of the guards, his own inherent worth and dignity. This was the real test of my beliefs. With each passing encounter, I saw the guards less and less as individuals. They were becoming a composite to me, all of them complicit in a complex system of evil. As they dehumanized me, I began to dehumanize them.

But every once in a while, the guards' attempts to dehumanize us backfired. Because so many of us had been arrested at once, the holding cells were at capacity — and that was before the stream of nighttime arrestees began arriving. All through the night, the guards herded different groups of us from one cell to another to another, ostensibly trying to balance the load. "Ten of you, come with me," a guard would order. The first time this happened, I found it unnerving because I didn't know where they were taking us. But I soon determined it served us well because we got to see and make connections with other protestors and hear their stories. And it wasn't long before their shuffling us around provided us with some much needed comic relief.

A guard opened the cell door and demanded, "Is Cindy Martinez in here?" When no one responded, she banged the door shut. We could hear her inquire in the next cell, and the next one. A little while later, another guard opened our door, and asked "Is Cindy Martinez in here?" She too, went from cell to cell in search of their prisoner. When a guard asked us for the third time whether Cindy Martinez was in our cell, several of us snickered under our breath.

After the guard closed the door again and was safely out of earshot, a woman sitting with her back to the door said in a low whisper, "Cindy's my cousin. She was transferred to Estrella sometime this morning. They don't know where she is." An almost imperceptible smirk came over her face. The rest of us broke into hysterics. If one of the goals of our civil disobedience was to disrupt Sheriff Joe's jail operations, we felt confident we had accomplished it. They couldn't even keep track of their own prisoners.

At one point, a young woman entered our cell. She looked around the room and, seeing several of us wearing the same yellow shirts, asked, "What's with the baseball team?"

I burst out laughing. "No, not baseball," I said, "We were involved in a protest today and they arrested us."

The woman's eyes lit up, her smile brightened, and she said, "You're the ones who were on TV! You shut down the jail! Let me shake your hands!" She then proceeded to move around the cell and shake the hands of every one of us wearing the shirts. "This is great," she went on, excitedly. "I can't wait to tell my people at home I was in here with you. You all are awesome." This woman knew that any day someone got something over on Sheriff Joe was a good day.

As part of yet another inmate shuffle, Susan Frederick-Gray and I eventually ended up in the same cell. My eyes went directly to her arms. *Were they injured?* They looked bruised, but the circular saw that terrified me earlier had not wounded her. I breathed a sigh of relief. She was shaken, but from her smile I could see she was not defeated.

Susan and I didn't know each other, but I wanted her to know how I appreciated her role in this action. She was, after all, the person who inspired me to be part of this campaign in the first place. "Thank you, Susan, for your courage out there," I said to her, as she maneuvered to find a place in the crowded holding cell.

"Thank *you*," she replied, smiling. "Thank you for coming. We couldn't have done this without all you who responded to our call." That was all that needed to be said between us.

Throughout the night, a steady stream of women who had not been a part of our actions were placed in our cell. Most were young and, of the those I talked with, most had been to jail before. But not for prostitution or drugs or the more serious crimes I imagined. The majority of the women I talked with were there for traffic offenses—traffic offenses that had snowballed uncontrollably until they had no choice but to work off their fines by spending time in jail. "We get fifty dollars off our fines for each day we spend in here," one woman told me—she had an unpaid speeding ticket that turned into a warrant, which resulted in a twelve hundred-dollar bill. "I took two weeks off work to spend fourteen days in here. When I get out, I will have cut my fine in half." For so many of these women, jail has become the new poorhouse.

I wrestled with the implications of this. She and so many like her are caught in a downward spiral from which there is no escape. This was driven home to me by one inmate, a woman of about fifty, her face covered with too much makeup, large breasts that were overexposed, and a body that could have also used a few more clothes. She arrived in our cell sometime late in the night. I don't remember her name or why she told us she got picked up, but I remember her as friendly. She engaged several of us in conversation. After a while, who knows how long, a guard opened the door and called her name. She got up, and when the guard said, "Come with me," she did. But something happened in the hallway. Other women who witnessed it said the guard told the woman to go into the adjacent cell, and when the woman turned around to look at her instead of immediately following the order, the guard slammed her head against the windowsill. All I heard was a loud thud, like an under-inflated basketball hitting the side of a house, hard—and then a single scream. It was more like a pain-filled grunt that emanated from deep in her gut as she crumbled to the floor. With my face pressed against the glass, I saw the blood—it spilled out in every direction like water from a sprinkler.

Other guards arrived quickly and got her out of there. I don't know where they took her. We never saw her again. What we saw next was that same prisoner from earlier in the night mopping up the blood. When he had cleaned the mess, the guard opened the cell door and moved the residents of that cell out into the hallway. The man then proceeded to use that same blood-soaked water to mop the floor of the cell before the guard directed its residents back into it.

I thought of that blood-soaked water on the cell floor when a lanky woman with tangled, brown, shoulder-length hair came in to our cell. She immediately retrieved the only roll of toilet paper in the cell. She lifted it above her head and with a circular motion of her wrist, emptied the roll, piece by piece, onto to the floor. *She must be mentally ill. What the heck is she doing?* I couldn't take my eyes off of her. Her wrist went round and round and round as the paper floated down to the floor. When she had emptied the roll, she tossed the empty roll in the trash can and lowered her body on to the paper, carefully so as not to disturb it. Like a mouse that had created a nest, she curled up her body and went to sleep in it. She had discovered her own way to shut out the craziness of this place. I wondered if I could ever adapt the way she had. I hoped I would never have to find out.

RELEASE

———◆———

Sometime during the night, Sheriff Joe came to visit us. A stocky man with glasses, a thinning hairline, broad nose, and noticeable gut, Arpaio fits the stereotypical appearance of a hard-hitting Western sheriff. Voters have reelected him five times since 1992, sometimes with as much as 83 percent of the vote. This is despite the proven fact that he routinely violates the constitutional rights of inmates and at the time of my arrest was being investigated by the U.S. Justice Department for racial profiling, unconstitutional policing, and retaliating against critics.

When informing us of Sheriff Joe's upcoming visit, one guard said, "He wants to see the people who have caused so much disruption to his jail."

I wanted to see the person whose jail we worked so hard to disrupt.

Who is this man who seems to have no compunction about treating human beings so harshly and yet, ironically, is an unabashed animal lover? The worst crime you can commit in Sheriff's Joe's eyes is not crossing the border illegally, or molesting a child, or even committing murder. The worst crime to Sheriff Joe is abusing an animal. Woe to the animal abuser who ends up in Sheriffs Joe's jail. In fact, he is so committed to animal rights that he converted the old jail building to a no-kill shelter for abused and neglected animals, especially intended for the animals of the people he arrests. He nurses the dogs, cats, and horses back to health, rehabilitates the vicious ones if he can, and finds good adoptive homes for those that are adoptable. The rest are welcome to live out the rest of their lives in his care. If only the humans in his care were so lucky.

Taped to the wall of our cell is a notice—the result of the most recent civil rights lawsuit—that the jail is required, among other things, to provide prisoners with a pillow and blanket if they have been in the holding cell for more than twenty-four hours. Earlier that evening, several of us advocated for one such prisoner. "I came in three days ago," she pleaded with the guards. "I need a blanket and pillow. I've got to get some sleep."

The guards denied her requests. "Shut up," they said. "You can't have been here that long."

Every time a guard opened the door for anything, we advocated on the woman's behalf. Finally, one guard admitted their mistake and passed the bedding in to her. "I checked the list. I guess you're right. Here, take this." And that was that.

Because one of the complaints in the lawsuit was about how hot it was inside the jail, I suspect that the jail's frigid temperature was an overreaction to that same lawsuit—as was the relentless balancing of the cell populations, with the theoretical goal of preventing overcrowding. The beating we had witnessed, however, was probably not consistent with the lawsuit's ruling.

The female protestors were divided among the three holding cells at the time of Sheriff's Joe's visit. I was in the last of the three cells, with my back pressed against the wall farthest from the door for support. We heard some commotion in the corridor. "It's Arpaio," one of the women exclaimed. Although we couldn't hear what he was saying through the glass, we could hear his voice as he talked to the women in the cell next to ours. All of a sudden, the women in the adjacent call started singing:

We shall overcome, we shall overcome,
We shall overcome someday.

Their voices quickly drowned out Arpaio's or any other voices. The sheriff and the two broad-shouldered men in suits accompanying him abruptly left that cell and approached ours. Before he had a chance to say anything to us, the women in my cell joined the chorus.

I understood the motivation to sing as a statement of defiance and resolve. After all, protest music had already steeled me for some tough moments on this journey. But I regretted missing the opportunity to talk with Sheriff Joe. I wanted to hear what he had to say, what he might ask us, and how he might respond to our questions. I wanted to ask him how he reconciled his treatment of humans with his treatment of animals. I wanted to ask how creating fear in the people he served was ever a solution. I wanted to ask why he was so afraid of people who were different from him.

Joe Arpaio, his jaw set and his brow furrowed, did not look pleased with our reception. He glared at us and then, without saying a word, did an about-face and left the area. His entourage followed.

We finished the verse we were on—yes, I had joined in—and the cell fell silent. I wondered out loud, "I wonder what he wanted to say to us." No one volunteered an idea. Maybe silencing him was the best thing to do. But I couldn't help wondering.

After an interminable night, Friday morning finally came—the time marked by the delivery of our peanut butter breakfast. After breakfast, we were shuffled around one more time. This time, all the female protestors were placed in one cell. "You'll be going to court in a couple of hours," one of the friendlier guards informed us. "We want you all in one place."

We were happy to be together, and someone started singing. This time, instead of a protest song, we sang,

"Spirit of Life," a reverent, prayerful hymn by Carolyn McDade, common in Unitarian Universalist congregations.

> Spirit of Life, come unto me.
> Sing in my heart all the stirrings of compassion.

After the hymn, we stood in a circle, holding hands, while Rev. Melissa Carville-Zimmer led us in prayer. I don't remember what she prayed but I know that with her words and the strength of the community around me, I began to let myself think about court. During the night, we had called Puente, the organization that was providing us with pro bono attorneys, and given them the list of people we knew had been arrested, but they had not told us anything. None of us had talked with an attorney. We had no idea what would happen in court, what we were supposed to do, or whether our attorneys would even be there. Although I was eager to get out of jail, I was also nervous about facing a judge, especially with no information.

Phoenix Municipal Court was conveniently located in the jail building, so we didn't have far to walk. A guard led us into the courtroom, motioned for us to take seats in the first three rows of plastic chairs, and instructed us to be quiet. At the end of the second row, an African-American woman sat huddled in a wheelchair, shaking uncontrollably, her arms folded tightly in front of her, her face muscles drawn tight. I recognized her as the woman I had encountered when I was arrested, the one whom police gave a second chance to decide whether she wanted to be arrested, the one who inspired me with her commitment to repay the sacrifice that others had given for her freedom. I was ashamed to admit that, consumed with my own situation, I had forgotten all about her. Several of the women hugged her and I saw her face relax. "I was so afraid," was all I could hear her say. I learned later that because she had trouble walking, she was placed in a wheelchair and put in isolation. Alone in the freezing cell all night, she could not use the toilet as she could not lift herself out of the wheelchair. The guards denied her any assistance, denied her pain medication, and of course denied her a blanket. She was terrified she would be forgotten.

"No talking," a guard admonished us once again.

We complied momentarily, but the volume of chatter rose out of control as one of the public defenders informed us that our attorneys had been delayed in security. "Don't worry," an older man in a rumpled suit, apparently one of the public defenders, said. "We can represent you."

A dark-haired woman wearing a Puente T-shirt turned to us and whispered, "Wait for the Puente attorneys. Don't let them handle your case. We don't know them." The rasp in her voice exposed her fear, but what were we to do? The judge would call the first case any minute now. My heart pounded so loudly that I was sure the judge would order me to quiet it.

Then another public defender, a matronly woman in a pale flowered dress, addressed us. "The prosecutor is offering a deal. Plead guilty and you'll get time served, no fines. And you won't have to come back to Phoenix for court."

The murmuring rose again in direct correlation to the anxiety among us. "I'm going to take it," one woman said. "I can't afford to come back." Another said, "We need to stick together. We don't have to take their plea." The woman from Puente pleaded with us, "Wait. Don't make any decisions. Our attorneys will be here. They'll know what to do."

"Quiet," the guard scolded. Again, we quieted down—for an instant.

As the judge entered the courtroom, so did our attorneys. Before the judge even sat down, one attorney addressed him, "Your honor, can we have a few minutes to talk with our clients?" The judge scanned the courtroom; it was filled to the brim. The male protestors had been required to exchange their "Love" T-shirts for prison garb, so they were indistinguishable from the other male prisoners, except perhaps for the absence of facial tattoos. We women still wore our protest garb. The judge looked frazzled by what lay ahead. I hoped that wasn't a bad sign.

"Bailiff," he inquired, "can we move some other cases forward so the counselors here can have a minute?"

"Yes, your honor," the bailiff replied swiftly, and he immediately called the first case. At least that part went smoothly. I could feel my heart pounding a little less forcefully.

With the first case under way, the four Puente attorneys conferred briefly with the two public defenders, and then all six of them started down the rows, kneeling in front of each of us, one at a time, to get our story. By the time one of them reached me, I had overhead the whispered conversations of several people ahead of me. That gave me the time and information I needed to decide what to do. I knew that by pleading not guilty, we would continue to cause disruption in the judicial system and have another opportunity to make a statement about why we did what we did. I had come this far. I might as well go all the way.

"Do you know how you want to plead?" the public defender asked.

"Yes, not guilty," I replied.

"You know that means you might have to come back. They might be able to hold the hearing over the phone but no guarantees."

"Yes. I'm prepared to come back, if I have to."

When my name was called, I stood with the public defender in front of the high bench on which the judge sat. "How do you plead?"

"Not guilty, your honor."

The district attorney pled his case, "Your honor, this woman is a transient, no known address. She can't be trusted to return to court. I recommend a five hundred-dollar bond."

The judge looked down at me, "Do you have an address?"

The attorney whispered to me that if I refused to give my address, I could be held in contempt. I had made the point I wanted to make at this juncture. I had helped disrupt Joe Arpaio's jail. I had helped shine light on his abuses. I was ready to go home. "Yes, sir," I replied, and proceeded to recite my North Carolina address.

The district attorney objected, in a sarcastic, angry tone, "Your honor, yesterday she was a transient. She must have just moved in overnight—while she was in jail. This is absurd."

The judge ignored his objection. "O.R.," he said, meaning I would be released on my own recognizance. "See the clerk to get your court date. Next case."

The district attorney literally threw his hands up in the air.

That was it. Even though I had no identification on me when I was arrested, I was released on my own recognizance. Without producing any proof, I was recognized by the judge as responsible, as trustworthy. This experience has confirmed what I believed to be true: as a white European American, I can stand in solidarity with but I cannot stand in the shoes of a person who is undocumented or who "looks" undocumented. My privilege shadows me everywhere.

I had expected to immediately walk out of the court a free person, but that was not the way it worked. We were escorted back to our cells. "Processing your release could take anywhere from two to eight hours," our escort informed us. When I heard that, my heart fell. I braced myself for a long wait. We were still in Sheriff Joe's house. I guess that meant he could keep us as long as he wanted.

But after only an hour or so, two guards took us down a long hallway and told us to wait there. A guard handed us each a piece of paper and ordered us to sign it, "Sign this form, then we'll give your stuff back."

"This form says we've received all of our stuff," one woman complained. "I'm not signing it until I get it back and I see it's all there."

"Sign the form, if you want to get out of here, or we can lock you back up, if you prefer that." Her message was clear. Forget what it says, just do as they say. We all signed the form.

Then they lined us up in the hallway and handed us the bags that contained our possessions: our water bottles, our shoelaces, our protest buttons. "Don't open the bags." the deputy ordered us. "You can't do that until you get outside." I clutched my possessions to me, relieved to have them back, relieved to know I would be free of this place soon.

Then, I heard chanting and cheering outside the front door. I couldn't make out what they were saying, but something deep inside of me told me they were there for us. The tension I had held inside me poured out. I braced myself on the wall so I wouldn't collapse from its release. I could feel their embrace. I could feel their love. How blessed I felt to not have to walk out of this building alone. How scary that must be for so many of those incarcerated with us. This was yet one more way we were different from those we came to stand with.

Across the hall from us, a lone woman, locked in a small cell, peered out of a tiny window, trying to see what all the commotion was about. The woman, with dark skin, jet black hair, and dark eyes, appeared young, probably in her late twenties. We had been told that these cells near the front were where they kept the undocumented—the "illegals." I suspected she was being processed to be turned over to U.S. Immigration and Customs Enforcement.

As she looked at us, Kat, the woman standing to my right, maneuvered one of the buttons in her bag to a place where it could be read through the clear plastic. She held it up to the woman. The woman struggled to read it—whether because of the size of the print, her level of literacy, or the language that was printed on it,

I couldn't tell. But she stayed with it, mouthing each word as she made it out.

No—human—is—illegal.

A radiant smile came across her face, almost as if a spotlight had been shown on her from above. She mouthed more words. This time the words came not from a button, but from her heart. "I love you," she said.

We smiled back at her. "We love you, too," Kat and I said in unison.

This was why we went through all this—what this whole journey was about. Justice isn't about changing laws, fixing abusive systems, or even getting rid of a corrupt sheriff. Justice is about ensuring that every person knows that he or she matters.

At that moment, I prayed that this woman realized how important she was, and I pray today that wherever she is, she still remembers.

EPILOGUE

---◆---

I never had to return to Phoenix. In January, seven months after our arrest, the charges against us were dropped. Because there were so many defendants, we were clustered into four different trials. I was scheduled for the last of the four trial dates. In the first trial, our attorneys argued that we couldn't be guilty of blocking an intersection because the police had already shut it down with their vehicles. They won their argument, and the defendants were acquitted. The district attorney was already angry that we hadn't accepted the plea bargain and had forced them to go to trial in the first place. Losing at trial was yet another embarrassment. They waited until the night before the second and third trials to drop the charges, which meant that the defendants had to travel back to Phoenix before learning they didn't have to go to court. I was spared that. They dropped my charges a week before I was scheduled to be there. I could finally breathe. It was over.

In looking back on an ordeal such as this, questions are inevitable. Was it worth it? What did we really accomplish? Would I do it again?

I do know that the Maricopa County Sheriff's Office was so overwhelmed with handling all of those arrested that Joe Arpaio was not able to conduct the massive raids on Latino communities that he had promised for the day that SB 1070 went into effect. In fact, we are told that because of all the media attention that resulted from the protests, it was several months before he resumed his raids. Most of the Unitarian Universalists who were arrested participated in a conference call in which we were interviewed by the U.S. Justice Department as part of its investigation into Arpaio's civil rights abuses. In December 2011, the U.S. Justice Department issued a report that charges Arpaio with engaging in "a pattern or practice of misconduct that violates the Constitution and federal law." I'd like to think that with the information we provided, we had a small hand in that.

Finally, we proved ourselves to be reliable partners to Latino organizations on the ground in Phoenix. We returned to Phoenix in June 2012 for the Unitarian Universalist General Assembly, the annual meeting of our denomination. Although none of us were arrested this time, thousands of us stood with our partners for, among other things, a protest against the ongoing civil and human rights abuses at Arpaio's Tent City jail.

Was it worth it? Absolutely. Would I do it again? I don't know. I'd like to think I could say yes, but knowing what to expect doesn't always make things easier. When I think about all the things that could go horribly wrong, I feel the hair rise on the back of my neck and a chill undulate through my body. Maybe this is the kind of thing Thomas Gray referred to when he said, "Where ignorance is bliss, 'tis folly to be wise." Wisdom comes at a price, and so does justice. I hope that if I'm asked again, I will remember the woman in the jail cell who told us she loved us and find it in me to do what needs to be done. In the meantime, I'm just happy to be home.